Oh Happy Day
LESSON PLANNER

AF120325

Teacher _____

School _____

Grade _____

Year _____

CONTENTS

How to Use the Lesson Planner 2

Substitute Teacher Information 4

Student Roster 6

Monthly Planner 8

Weekly Lesson Plans 32

Celebrating Birthdays 112

Teacher Created Resources
12621 Western Avenue
Garden Grove, CA 92841
www.teachercreated.com
ISBN: 978-1-4206-8321-9
©2021 Teacher Created Resources
Made in U.S.A.

Editor in Chief: Karen Goldfluss, M.S. Ed.

Creative Director: Sarah M. Fournier

Cover Design: Diem Pascarella

Imaging: Diem Pascarella

Publisher: Mary D. Smith, M.S. Ed.

The classroom teacher may reproduce the materials in this book for use in a single classroom only. The reproduction of any part of this book for other classrooms or for an entire school or school system is strictly prohibited. No part of this publication may be transmitted or recorded in any form without written permission from the publisher with the exception of electronic material, which may be stored on the purchaser's computer only.

©Teacher Created Resources, Inc. #8321 Lesson Planner

How to Use the Lesson Planner

 Substitute Teacher Information (pages 4–5)

Document all pertinent information on these pages. If you have a copy of the layout of your school, attach it to page 5. Be sure to show important locations, such as the office, restrooms, faculty lounge, cafeteria, auditorium, and playground. Photocopy these pages, and give a copy to your school office manager, instructional assistant, or a grade-level team member.

 Student Roster (pages 6–7)

Use the roster to record information for each student. Having the roster in your lesson planner provides you with quick and easy access to important data for both you and a substitute teacher.

 Monthly Planning (pages 8–31)

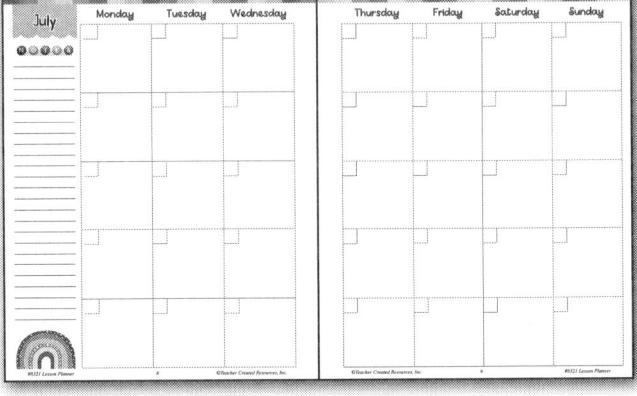

In addition to the weekly lesson plan pages in this book, you will find blank calendar pages for year-long planning. They can be used to note special plans, weekly/monthly meetings and appointments, and other useful information throughout the year. The first column may be used for notes and to list monthly priorities. You may wish to reproduce each month, add important information for the class, and then post the calendar months on a bulletin board or other display. Include special events, positive sayings, inspirational quotes, and friendly reminders for each calendar month.

 Weekly Lesson Plans (pages 32–111)

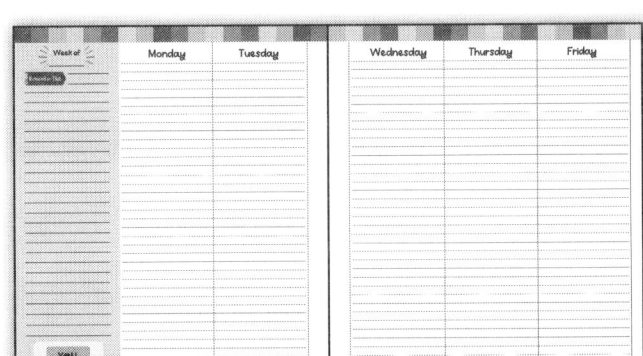

Use this section to help you organize your lesson plans each week. There are enough weekly plan pages to cover a 40-week school year. At the top of the left-hand page, fill in the blank to indicate the week dates for which the plans are written. For special programs requiring more in-depth explanations, you may wish to reference a specific folder, notebook, guide, etc., for more information. This information can be very helpful to substitute teachers.

 Celebrating Birthdays (page 112)

Whether you celebrate birthdays in a big way or your birthday acknowledgements are more simple, students enjoy the recognition on this special day. Keep track of students' birthdays with the handy chart on this page.

 Super Sticker Stuff

Personalize your Lesson Planner with the colorful and functional stickers provided. This is a great way to highlight your everyday routines and help you keep track of special events and reminders in your busy schedule. The stickers are designed to fit the daily columns of your weekly lesson pages, but you can also be creative in your placements. After all, this is your planner!

#8321 Lesson Planner — ©Teacher Created Resources, Inc.

How to Use the Lesson Planner

This seating chart is provided for easy reference. Table and desk arrangements will vary throughout the year depending on room size, available furniture, grade level taught, teaching style, and academic program needs. To accommodate a variety of classroom arrangements, you may wish to create additional charts and place specific seating information in a separate folder.

Substitute Teacher Information

● We're here to help!

Helpful Students

_____
_____
_____
_____

Teachers

_____
_____
_____

Principal

_____

Office Manager

_____

Maintenance

_____

● In Case of Emergency

Support Staff _____

First Aid Kit Location _____

Fire Extinguisher Location _____

Class Emergency Meeting Spot _____

● Teacher Duties

_____
_____
_____
_____
_____
_____
_____
_____
_____

#8321 Lesson Planner ©*Teacher Created Resources, Inc.*

Substitute Teacher Information

● Procedures to Note

● Special Needs Students

Daily Schedule

Class Begins	
Morning Recess	
Lunch	
Class Resumes	
Afternoon Recess	
Dismissal	

Student Roster

	Student	Parent/Guardian	Address
1.			
2.			
3.			
4.			
5.			
6.			
7.			
8.			
9.			
10.			
11.			
12.			
13.			
14.			
15.			
16.			
17.			
18.			
19.			
20.			
21.			
22.			
23.			
24.			
25.			
26.			
27.			
28.			
29.			
30.			
31.			
32.			
33.			
34.			
35.			
36.			

 Student Roster

Home Phone	Cell Phone	Work Phone	Notes

July

NOTES

	Sunday	Monday	Tuesday

Wednesday	Thursday	Friday	Saturday

Wednesday	Thursday	Friday	Saturday

August

NOTES

Sunday	Monday	Tuesday

#8321 Lesson Planner   ©Teacher Created Resources, Inc.

Wednesday	Thursday	Friday	Saturday

September

NOTES

Sunday	Monday	Tuesday

#8321 Lesson Planner

Wednesday	Thursday	Friday	Saturday

©Teacher Created Resources, Inc.   #8321 Lesson Planner

October

NOTES

Sunday	Monday	Tuesday

#8321 Lesson Planner

Wednesday	Thursday	Friday	Saturday

©Teacher Created Resources, Inc.   #8321 Lesson Planner

November

NOTES

	Sunday	Monday	Tuesday

#8321 Lesson Planner · ©Teacher Created Resources, Inc.

Wednesday	Thursday	Friday	Saturday

December

NOTES

Sunday	Monday	Tuesday

#8321 Lesson Planner · ©Teacher Created Resources, Inc.

Wednesday	Thursday	Friday	Saturday

©Teacher Created Resources, Inc.   #8321 Lesson Planner

January

NOTES

Sunday	Monday	Tuesday

Wednesday	Thursday	Friday	Saturday

February

NOTES

Sunday	Monday	Tuesday

#8321 Lesson Planner

Wednesday	Thursday	Friday	Saturday

©Teacher Created Resources, Inc.   #8321 Lesson Planner

March

NOTES

Sunday	Monday	Tuesday

#8321 Lesson Planner

Wednesday	Thursday	Friday	Saturday

©*Teacher Created Resources, Inc.* — *#8321 Lesson Planner*

April

NOTES

Sunday	Monday	Tuesday

#8321 Lesson Planner

Wednesday	Thursday	Friday	Saturday

May

NOTES

Sunday	Monday	Tuesday

Wednesday	Thursday	Friday	Saturday

©Teacher Created Resources, Inc.   #8321 Lesson Planner

June

NOTES

Sunday	Monday	Tuesday

#8321 Lesson Planner

Wednesday	Thursday	Friday	Saturday

Week of _____

Remember This

today is YOURS

Monday

Tuesday

Wednesday	Thursday	Friday

Week of _____

Remember This

Just do your THING

Monday	Tuesday

Wednesday	Thursday	Friday

Week of
_____

Remember This

Monday

Tuesday

Clear Skies AHEAD

#8321 Lesson Planner

Wednesday	Thursday	Friday

Week of _____

Remember This

Monday	Tuesday

Sunshine and Happy times

Wednesday	Thursday	Friday

Week of _____

Remember This

Monday

Tuesday

#8321 Lesson Planner

CREATE your own RAINBOW

©Teacher Created Resources, Inc.

Wednesday	Thursday	Friday

Week of _____

Remember This

Monday	Tuesday

LIVE LIFE in COLOR

Wednesday	Thursday	Friday

Week of _____

Remember This

Monday	Tuesday

Hello Sunshine

Wednesday	Thursday	Friday

Week of _____

Remember This

Be the SUNSHINE

#8321 Lesson Planner

Monday	Tuesday

Wednesday	Thursday	Friday

Week of _____

Remember This

Monday

Tuesday

Let's do THIS

Wednesday	Thursday	Friday

Week of
_____

Remember This

Monday	Tuesday

YOU are all KiNDS OF Amazing

Wednesday	Thursday	Friday

Week of _____

Remember This _____

Now is a GOOD time

#8321 Lesson Planner

Monday

Tuesday

Wednesday	Thursday	Friday

Week of _____

Remember This

Monday

Tuesday

Make it RAIN Rainbows

Wednesday	Thursday	Friday

Week of _____

Remember This

Get It DONE

Monday	Tuesday

Wednesday	Thursday	Friday

Week of _____

Remember This

STAY inspired

#8321 Lesson Planner

Monday	Tuesday

Wednesday	Thursday	Friday

Week of _____

Remember This

today is YOURS

#8321 Lesson Planner

Monday

Tuesday

©Teacher Created Resources, Inc.

Wednesday	Thursday	Friday

Week of _____

Remember This

Just do your THING

Monday	Tuesday

Wednesday	Thursday	Friday

Week of
_____

Remember This

Monday	Tuesday

#8321 Lesson Planner

Clear Skies AHEAD

©Teacher Created Resources, Inc.

Wednesday	Thursday	Friday

Week of _____

Remember This

Monday

Tuesday

Sunshine and Happy times

Wednesday	Thursday	Friday

Week of _____

Remember This

Monday

Tuesday

Create your own Rainbow

Wednesday	Thursday	Friday

Week of _____

Remember This

Monday	Tuesday

LIVE LIFE in COLOR

#8321 Lesson Planner ©Teacher Created Resources, Inc.

Wednesday	Thursday	Friday

Week of
_____

Remember This

Monday	Tuesday

#8321 Lesson Planner

Wednesday	Thursday	Friday

Week of _____

Remember This

Monday

Tuesday

Be the SUNSHINE

#8321 Lesson Planner

Wednesday	Thursday	Friday

Week of _____

Remember This

Let's do THIS

Monday	Tuesday

Wednesday	Thursday	Friday

Week of _____

Remember This _____

Monday

Tuesday

#8321 Lesson Planner

Wednesday	Thursday	Friday

Week of _____

Remember This

Now is a GOOD time

#8321 Lesson Planner

Monday

Tuesday

Wednesday	Thursday	Friday

Week of _____

Remember This

Make it RAIN Rainbows

Monday	Tuesday

Wednesday	Thursday	Friday

Week of _____

Remember This

Get It DONE

#8321 Lesson Planner

Monday

Tuesday

Wednesday	Thursday	Friday

Week of
_____

Remember This

STAY inspired

#8321 Lesson Planner

Monday

Tuesday

86 ©Teacher Created Resources, Inc.

Wednesday	Thursday	Friday

Week of _____

Remember This

Monday

Tuesday

today is YOURS

Wednesday	Thursday	Friday

Week of _____

Remember This

Monday

Tuesday

Just do your THING

Wednesday	Thursday	Friday

Week of _____

Remember This

Clear Skies AHEAD

Monday	Tuesday

Wednesday	Thursday	Friday

Week of _____

Remember This

Monday

Tuesday

Sunshine and Happy times

Wednesday	Thursday	Friday

©Teacher Created Resources, Inc.   #8321 Lesson Planner

Week of _____

Remember This

Monday	Tuesday

CREATE your own RAINBOW

Wednesday	Thursday	Friday

Week of _____

Remember This

Monday

Tuesday

Live Life in Color

#8321 Lesson Planner

Wednesday	Thursday	Friday

Week of
_____

Remember This

Monday	Tuesday

HELLO SUNSHINE

#8321 Lesson Planner
©Teacher Created Resources, Inc.

Wednesday	Thursday	Friday

Week of
_____

Remember This

Monday	Tuesday

Be the SUNSHINE

#8321 Lesson Planner

Wednesday	Thursday	Friday

Week of
_____

Remember This

Let's do THIS

Monday	Tuesday

Wednesday	Thursday	Friday

Week of _____

Remember This

YOU are all KiNDS OF Amazing

Monday	Tuesday

Wednesday	Thursday	Friday

Week of
_____

Remember This

Now is a GOOD time

Monday	Tuesday

Wednesday	Thursday	Friday

Week of _____

Remember This

Make it RAIN Rainbows

Monday	Tuesday

Wednesday	Thursday	Friday

Celebrating Birthdays

January

February

March

April

May

June

July

August

September

October

November

December